*VIZIER RAMOSE carved in hieroglyphs.*
*Relief from his tomb.* Photograph by Alfred Tamarin

# The Mummy of Ramose

# Other Books
## By SHIRLEY GLUBOK

Art and Archaeology
The Art of Africa
The Art of America from Jackson
  to Lincoln
The Art of America in the Early
  Twentieth Century
The Art of America in the Gilded
  Age
The Art of America Since World
  War II
The Art of Ancient Egypt
The Art of Ancient Greece
The Art of Ancient Mexico
The Art of Ancient Peru
The Art of Ancient Rome
The Art of China
The Art of Colonial America
The Art of India
The Art of Japan
The Art of Lands in the Bible

The Art of the Eskimo
The Art of the Estruscans
The Art of the New American Nation
The Art of the North American Indian
The Art of the Northwest Coast Indians
The Art of the Old West
The Art of the Plains Indians
The Art of the Southwest Indians
The Art of the Spanish in the
  United States and Puerto Rico
The Art of the Woodland Indians
The Fall of the Aztecs
The Fall of the Incas
Dolls Dolls Dolls
Digging in Assyria
Discovering the Royal Tombs at Ur
Discovering Tut-Ankh-Amen's Tomb
Home and Child Life in Colonial Days
Knights in Armour

## By SHIRLEY GLUBOK and ALFRED TAMARIN

Ancient Indians of the Southwest
Olympic Games in Ancient Greece

Voyaging to Cathay: Americans in
  the China Trade

## By ALFRED TAMARIN

The Autobiography of Benvenuto
  Cellini
Benjamin Franklin: An Auto-
  biographical Portrait
Fire Fighting in America

Japan and the United States: The Early
  Encounters
Revolt in Judea: The Road to Masada
We Have Not Vanished: Eastern
  Indians of the United States

*Funeral ceremonies at entrance to a tomb. Wall painting
from Tomb of Nebamun and Ipuky.* The Metropolitan Museum of Art,
photograph by Egyptian Expedition

# The Mummy of Ramose

## THE LIFE AND DEATH OF AN ANCIENT EGYPTIAN NOBLEMAN

Shirley Glubok and Alfred Tamarin

HARPER & ROW, PUBLISHERS
New York, Hagerstown, San Francisco, London

Library of Congress Cataloging in Publication Data
Glubok, Shirley.
    The mummy of Ramose.

    SUMMARY: Describes the life of an Egyptian nobleman
of the Eighteenth Dynasty and mummification and funeral
rites that followed his death.
    1. Mummies—Juvenile literature.    2. Funeral rites
and ceremonies—Egypt—Juvenile literature.    3. Ramose—
Juvenile literature.    4. Egypt—Nobility—Biography—
Juvenile literature.    [1. Mummies.    2. Funeral rites
and ceremonies—Egypt.    3. Ramose.    4. Egypt—History—
To 332 B.C.]    I. Tamarin, Alfred H., joint author.
II. Title.
DT62.M7G58    932'.01'0924 [B]    76–21392
ISBN 0–06–022039–2
ISBN 0–06–022042–2 lib. bdg.

# Contents

1  The Morning of Ramose's Last Day  1

2  The Rise and Fall of Ramose  4

3  The Life-Giving Nile  16

4  The Legend of Osiris  20

5  In the Tomb  28

6  The Evening of Ramose's Last Day  37

7  Death on the Roof  45

8  Mummification and Funeral Rites  49

Postscript  71

Selected Bibliography  75

Index  77

# The Mummy of Ramose

# 1 The Morning of Ramose's Last Day

Beyond the eastern horizon, the darkness of the night sky faded ever so slightly, leaving behind the black shadow of the desert mountains. A new day was dawning, the day when Ramose, formerly Grand Vizier of Egypt, chief counselor of two Egyptian Pharaohs, would die.

In the dim predawn light, Ramose left his palace in Thebes and was carried slowly through the dusty streets in his litter, a chair supported by poles on the shoulders of four servants. He was on his way to the desert cliffs on the west bank of the Nile River, where his wife, Meritptah, was buried. Her mummified body lay in a hidden rock chamber cut into the side of a barren cliff.

As the litter swayed with the movement of his carriers, Ramose's mind filled with warm memories of his dead wife. How fond he had been of the dainty "Enchantress of Amun," as Meritptah had been called. Amun was the rich and powerful god of Thebes, and chief of all the divinities of Egypt.

Ramose had expected that his wife, who had been much younger than he, would outlive him, but now she was dead. Every morning since her burial, he had crossed the Nile to visit the rock-chamber tomb, which he intended to share with Meritptah as their "House of Eternity." Every morning he had taken part in memorial ceremonies and had stood before the stone sarcophagus containing the coffins with her mummified body.

Ramose's litter reached his boat, and he climbed on board. On deck, under a canopy, a chair was ready for him. As he took his seat, the craft swung into the tide of the river and, with the help of oars, moved silently toward the western bank. A boatman standing in the stern steered the vessel skillfully. In the center of the craft, a sail on the single mast was unfurled to

catch any puff of wind that might help speed the crossing. A watchman in the prow kept an eye on the numerous other boats plying the river even at this early hour of the morning. Barges laden with goods poked along, and small papyrus boats carrying families darted in and out. A light wind from the desert filled the sail on Ramose's boat, and the prow slid into the early morning mist.

*Boats on the Nile. Wall painting from Tomb of Sennufer.*
The Metropolitan Museum of Art, photograph by Egyptian Expedition

# 2 The Rise and Fall of Ramose

As the most important official in all Egypt, second only to the divine Pharaoh himself, Ramose had crossed the Nile thousands of times over the years. Now he was an old man, with no state duties to perform.

Ramose, who was from a most distinguished Egyptian family, had risen to become one of the two chief counselors, or viziers, of King Amenhotep III. He was the vizier of the Pharaoh in Thebes, capital of Southern Egypt. Ramose's cousin, Amenhotep-son-of-Hapu, an architect whose learning was to become legend, was the King's Scribe and had been Overseer of All Works of the King. Another cousin, who was the father of Ramose's wife, had earlier been the king's vizier in Memphis, the capital of Northern Egypt, as had Meritptah's brother, who had succeeded his father to the post.

Ramose's cousins had seen that he was a young man of promise and had helped him rise in government service. When he was eighteen years old, they had taken him to the coronation of Amenhotep III's father, Thutmosis IV. At this splendid ceremony, the new king wore the double crown, representing the uniting of Upper and Lower Egypt, an event which had occurred around 3100 B.C. The union of the two lands had marked the beginning of the first dynastic period. A dynasty is a series of kings from the same family, who rule one after another, for generations. Ramose lived during the Eigh-

*Palette of Narmer,
front and back view,
illustrating the conquest
of the north and
the Unification of
Upper and Lower Egypt.*
Cairo Museum

teenth Dynasty, which lasted from about 1570 to 1320 B.C. during the period now called The New Kingdom.

The coronation of Thutmosis IV had taken place almost forty years earlier, in a year now estimated to have been about 1425 B.C. After he was crowned king, Thutmosis married Mutemwiya, a princess of the Asiatic realm of Mitanni. Ramose could vividly remember the excitement of the wedding and the magnificent gifts from the bride's father. Yet in the midst of rejoicing over this alliance with such a powerful king, the Egyptian priests had whispered that the bride, a foreign princess with no royal Egyptian blood, could not pass down to a son the legitimate right to rule.

Soon after their marriage, the young princess Mutemwiya had given birth to a baby boy. Unfortunately, the infant had died and been laid to rest in the tomb which was being prepared for his father. Kings and other important Egyptians spent years preparing their own tombs. A second child, a girl, had also died in her cradle and been interred in her father's tomb.

Almost immediately after Thutmosis IV ascended the throne, his wife gave birth to another son, who was named Prince Amenhotep. When Thutmosis died and the youngster ascended the throne at the age of nine, the priests muttered that his blood was impure, and they doubted his right to be Pharaoh. The child took as his throne name Neb-maet-ra Amenhotep, which means "Amun is satisfied." He was the third Pharaoh to have that name. During his reign, which

*Amenhotep III.*
British Museum

lasted more than thirty-five years, Egypt reached heights of splendor never dreamed of before, and Amenhotep III became known as "Amenhotep the Magnificent."

Ramose and his high-ranking relatives helped Amenhotep III realize his vast building projects. Additions were made to the enormous temple at Karnak, dedicated to Amun, which had been started by predecessors of the young Pharaoh about five hundred years before. From start to finish the temple would take about two thousand years to build. The Temple of Amun at Karnak was to become the largest religious structure in the ancient world. One of its spectacular features was its

long avenues lined with sphinxes. A sphinx is a figure with the body of a crouching lion and the head of a king, showing that the king is as strong as a lion.

On the west bank of the Nile, Amenhotep-son-of-Hapu built for the Pharaoh a mortuary temple, dedicated to the celebration of funeral rites. In front of it stone figures were set up, which became known as the Colossi of Memnon. The Pharaoh expressed his gratitude by granting a tomb and mortuary temple for his architect near the royal tombs, in what is now known as the Valley of the Kings, on the west bank of the Nile.

*Colossi of Memnon.*
The Metropolitan Museum of Art, David Hunter McAlpin Fund, 1966, photograph by Francis Frith, 1857

Amenhotep III also ordered the building of a new temple dedicated to Amun, in Thebes, near the royal palace, on the east bank of the river, in what is now the modern town of Luxor. His purpose was to please the priests and silence their gossip about his foreign blood. The beautiful new temple of Amun so satisfied the priests that they finally stopped questioning the right of Amenhotep's mother to be called "Mother of a King."

When he had ascended the throne, the nine-year-old King Amenhotep III had immediately been married to a four-year-old bride named Teye. The young girl grew into womanhood and gave birth to a boy, Thutmosis. This first royal son lived only long enough to be given titles such as High Priest of Ptah. Ptah was god of Memphis. Soon afterward the court celebrated the birth of a daughter, who was named Sitamun. Years later Sitamun was married to Amenhotep III, her own father, to keep the royal bloodline pure. It was common in Egyptian royal households for kings to marry young princesses within their own families to preserve the royal line, and it was not unusual for kings to marry their own daughters.

The court rejoiced again when Queen Teye gave birth to another son, who was named Amenhotep. The father decided that when his son became old enough, he would share the throne and become co-regent. The prince was a strange child, with a bulging cranium, large chin and thin neck. His body was misshapen, with a round belly, sloping shoulders and large thighs. The father had been a mighty hunter in his youth, but the son was physically weak. A lonely lad, he wandered through

*Queen Teye.*
Egyptian Museum,
West Berlin

*Temple at Luxor.*
Courtesy Lehnert and Landrock, Cairo

the corridors of the palace, brooding.

Young Prince Amenhotep married his cousin Nefertiti, whose name means "a beautiful woman has come." He was also given a harem of lesser wives and concubines, but she was his chief wife. Nefertiti's family was close to the throne. Her father, Ay, was King's Lieutenant of Chariotry and Master of the Horse.

When the prince ascended the throne as Amenhotep IV, co-regent with his father, Ramose was asked to serve as chief counselor to both rulers. The two Pharaohs ruled jointly for eleven years. Even though Ramose was vizier to both father and son, he never really understood the younger Amenhotep, whose eyes were constantly turned to the heavens, studying the sun moving across the sky. The young king seemed fascinated with the blazing orb. In the morning he watched the fiery red ball float out from behind the eastern horizon with a sudden burst of light. In Egypt, dawn is swift; the shadows of the night pull away from the hills quickly, and the sun's rays reach out to embrace the land. In the evening, the bright ball of the sun seems to hesitate over the western edge of the earth; then suddenly it dips behind the rim of the hills like an orange balloon pulled by an invisible cord. Twilight is brief. The curtain of night is drawn swiftly across the desert and over the narrow bands of green fields on both banks of the Nile.

The strong influence of the sun on the young Pharaoh puzzled Ramose. Soon it was on everyone's lips that the young Amenhotep believed that the Aten, a new form of sun-god, was even more powerful than the ancient Amun, the god whom the Egyptians had worshipped for centuries. Unlike other Egyptian gods, who took the forms of animals and people, the Aten was represented as a sun disk.

The young Pharaoh, breaking with age-old beliefs of his ancestors, had a temple built in Karnak dedicated to his new god. But Thebes, the capital, was under the tight control of the priests of Amun. So the young Amenhotep convinced his father that a new city should be built. The new city, called Akhetaten, which means "the Horizon of Aten," was hastily constructed in two years. The site, almost three hundred miles to the north of the old capital at Thebes, is now called Tell el Amarna. At Akhetaten, a palace was constructed with royal

*Gold statuette of Amun from the temple of Amun at Karnak.*
The Metropolitan Museum of Art,
Gift of Edward S. Harkness, 1926

*Akhenaten and Nefertiti with three daughters under the rays of Aten.*
From Tell el Amarna. Egyptian Museum, West Berlin

apartments and a great court where the young king and his
family could worship their only god, the Aten, in full sunlight.
Amenhotep IV changed his own name to Akhenaten, which
means "the spirit of the Aten."

When Akhenaten transferred his court to the new city, the

young Pharaoh's stewards, ministers, generals and courtiers went along with him. Most of them were the sons of officials who had served his father. The aging Vizier Ramose was not invited to go along to the new capital; he stayed behind in Thebes and continued as vizier to the ailing Amenhotep III. Sadly he watched the glory of the old capital fade. When Amenhotep the Magnificent died at the age of forty-seven, in the thirty-eighth year of his reign, Ramose yielded his office in Thebes to a younger man.

Since the death of Amenhotep III, time had seemed endless to Ramose. With no official duties to perform and without his beloved wife, and with no children to comfort him and help him pass the lonely hours, he found the days empty and silent.

# 3 The Life-Giving Nile

As Ramose stepped off his boat onto the western bank of the Nile, he could see men planting in the fields. The Egyptians, who were among the world's first farmers, began to practice agriculture around seven thousand years ago. Wheat, barley, onions, beans and flax, which is used to make linen, were grown along the Nile. The Egyptians were also among the first people to practice irrigation. As early as 5000 B.C., Egyptian farmers were using water from the Nile to irrigate their fields.

The Nile, the longest river in the world, starts in the African highlands. This river runs through Egypt for about 940 miles, from the First Cataract, or rapid, in the south, at Aswan, to the Mediterranean Sea, where it empties. As the Nile flows northward through Egypt, it cuts a cleft into the Sahara plateau, creating a winding ribbon of land hemmed in by limestone cliffs. About a hundred miles before it reaches the Mediterranean, the river opens out into many branches, forming a broad, fan-shaped area, or delta, about 150 miles wide at the sea.

The regular rising of the waters of the Nile provided the only moisture for the crops in Egypt. This hot country, where there was no rainfall, was entirely dependent for its agriculture on the annual flooding of the river. Keeping track of the seasons was vital to Ramose, as the Pharaoh's Vizier of Upper Egypt. Southern Egypt is considered Upper Egypt, because the Nile

16

begins in the mountains in the south and flows northward, emptying into the sea.

Often, in the dry months of the year, before the floods came, Ramose would watch the soil crack with thirst under the blazing sun, as the level of water in the river sank lower and lower. Then each summer the annual miracle took place. Waters from melting snows in the far-off mountains and from heavy tropical rains which had fallen to the south, where the Nile begins, came swelling down the river. The water, filled with sediments of organic matter and minerals, which made rich fertilizer, continued rising throughout the summer, submerging the land. Ramose, like all Egyptians for thousands of years, rejoiced at the flood of life-giving water. When the floods receded, narrow ribbons of fertile land were left behind on both sides of the river. The rising and falling of the Nile reenacted the miracle of Creation for the ancient Egyptians, who believed that the world began when a mound of earth arose from the depths of the ocean.

News of the river's rising and falling were of vital importance to Ramose as chief counselor for the Pharaohs. Careful measurements were taken of the water level as it rose, and word was rushed to him. If the flood was low, spelling a "meager" Nile for the year, there would be "the year of the hyena," which meant hardship and famine for the three million people who lived in Egypt. If the flood proved excessive, care had to be taken to prevent the water from overflowing the canals or washing away the dikes which helped store the water until it was needed for the parched fields. Ramose's men would make

17

*Farming scenes. Wall painting from Tomb of Nakht.*
The Metropolitan Museum of Art, photograph by Egyptian Expedition

frequent tours of inspection to be sure that the dikes and reservoirs were in good condition. A "good Nile," with sufficient water and an easy flood, forecast peace and prosperity for everybody.

The first day of inundation usually coincided with the rising of Sirius, the Dog Star, in mid-July. The appearance of Sirius was observed as New Year's Day by the Egyptians. The Season of Inundation lasted for about four months. Inundation was followed by the Season of Germination and the Warm Season, when the waters would gradually subside.

As the floodwaters drained away, leaving behind the rich silt that made the soil fertile, seeds were sown. In the Season of Germination, the seeds under the ground would begin to stir with new life. In the Warm Season, which followed, the grain, nurtured by the sun, would grow tall. As the fields turned green, then golden, the crops were measured. Finally the crops ripened and were ready for the harvest. The size of the harvest was noted and the herds of cattle were counted and dutifully recorded by scribes. These reports perhaps led to the development of the earliest form of Egyptian writing, which used picture symbols known as hieroglyphs.

# 4 The Legend of Osiris

As Ramose continued his journey to his wife's tomb, the Nile was receding; the land was emerging and insects and birds were returning. When Ramose's litter reached the tomb the sun had come up over the eastern hills. The entrance to the tomb was hidden in the side of a cliff. In earlier times it had been the practice for Egyptian kings to be buried in pyramids: enormous stone structures, square at the base and tapering to a point at the top. Noblemen had been buried in mastabas, which have rectangular bases with sloping sides and a flat roof. But these old, massive burial structures were so visible they were broken into, and the precious contents were carried off.

Thutmosis I, in an attempt to hide his burial place from robbers, searched for the most inaccessible location on the west bank of the Nile, in what is now known as the Valley of the Kings. He carved his tomb out of the rocky hills along a remote gorge in the barren mountains and hid the entrance under desert sand, leaving no visible structure to attract greedy grave robbers. In order not to betray the location of his tomb, Thutmosis built his mortuary temple a distance away from the grave site. Formerly, mortuary temples had been built next to the tombs.

Other, later Pharaohs also had their burial places cut into the sides of cliffs in the Valley of the Kings. Nearby, important officials such as Ramose carved out of the rock their own final resting places. Ramose's tomb was not as large as a royal tomb. It was more or less an underground version of the houses that Theban noblemen lived in.

The entrance to Ramose's tomb faces the rising sun, so the first rays fall on the doorway. Ramose walked down the steps. In the center of the steps was an inclined ramp onto which a stone sarcophagus could be easily lowered. He went through the large courtyard, which had been cut in an irregular shape to avoid other tombs that had been dug above and around it. Moving along, he entered a great hall with thirty-two columns carved from floor to ceiling out of the

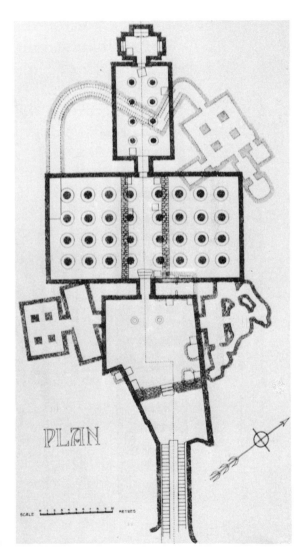

PLAN

SCALE          METRES

*Ground plan of Tomb of Ramose.* From *The Tomb of Ramose* by Norman de Garis Davis, Egypt Exploration Society

living rock, in the shape of papyrus plants. These columns were thick and sturdy and served as solid supports for the immense weight of the roof. A corridor led from the main hall down to the burial chamber 55 feet below the surface.

Ramose walked through the inner hall with its eight smaller columns and joined the priests, who were waiting for him in the shrine. As soon as the nobleman arrived, the priests began the ceremony called the "Mortuary Liturgy," which was conducted for the vizier's dead wife.

Ramose and the priests bowed before a small statue of Meritptah, which stood in a niche. They picked up the image and placed it on a mound of sand, then purified it with sacred oil. The nobleman took the carved image, cradled it in his arms, dressed it in a colorful robe and went through the motions of feeding it. Then the priests anointed the mouth and eyes of the statue with sacred oil, before touching its lips with a hooked instrument. This part of the ceremony, called the "Opening of the Mouth," was intended to restore to Meritptah the use of her arms, body, legs and senses. The Opening of the Mouth recalled the rites that were said to have been performed for the god Osiris by his son Horus.

According to legend, Osiris was a king of Egypt, a wise and capable ruler. One day he went on a trip to a distant province, leaving his wife Isis, who was also his sister, to look after the kingdom. Osiris' younger brother Seth was in love with their sister, Isis. Jealous of the king, Seth made up his mind to usurp the throne; he decided to have his brother murdered. He invited Osiris to a great banquet on his return from his travels. During the feast a large coffer, made of wonderful woods and decorated with precious metals and magnificent jewels, was brought to the banquet hall. Seth announced that this box would be presented to the guest who fit into it exactly. One by one, seventy-two guests stretched themselves to their full lengths inside the coffer, but everyone proved to be too short. At last Osiris lay down inside the beautiful box, and it fit him as though it had been measured for him. Quickly Seth shut the lid and fastened it down, so that Osiris could not escape. The coffer was then covered with lead and cast into the Nile.

Miraculously, the heavy box containing the body of Osiris did not sink. It floated downstream, into the Mediterranean, and across the sea to the coast of Syria, where it was washed ashore near Byblos in Phoenicia. There it lay among the branches of a tamarisk tree. The tree quickly grew and enclosed the box within its trunk. The king of the country admired the tree and had it cut down to make a pillar to hold up the roof of his house.

All the while, Osiris' wife, Isis, had been searching desperately for her husband. When she finally learned where his body could be found, she sailed across the Mediterranean to Byblos. There she became a nursemaid to one of the royal children in the court of the queen, Ishtar. In time Isis revealed her identity to Ishtar and begged to be given the pillar containing the body of Osiris. Ishtar granted her request, and Isis recovered the coffer, then sailed back home with it.

Isis took Osiris' body to a hiding place in the marshes of the Nile Delta, where she thought it would be safe from the vengeful eyes of Seth. There the seed of her dead husband was miraculously implanted in her womb, and a son was born, who was given the name Horus.

Meanwhile, Seth had also been searching for the body of his murdered brother. Finally he learned that it was being guarded by Isis in a secret hiding place. One day when Isis was absent, Seth found the coffer in the marshes and carried it off. He removed his brother's corpse from the box, hacked it into dozens of pieces and scattered the parts far and wide over the land. Isis was shocked by the treachery of her younger brother. With the help of the goddess Nepthys she patiently hunted for every section of her husband's body, and carefully collected and reassembled them. Then Osiris' body was mummified.

According to legend, Osiris was the first Egyptian to be mummified, that is, his body was preserved by being embalmed, then wrapped in many layers of linen. Egyptians believed that life would continue even after death as long as the physical body was kept from decaying. It was the jackal-headed god Anubis, the divine embalmer, who mummified Osiris. Thereafter, everybody who was mummified was said to be reunited with Osiris. Osiris is represented as an upright mummy, holding the crook and flail, symbols of kingship.

When Isis' son, Horus, came of age, he set out to avenge the murder of his father. Horus' Uncle Seth never knew about his birth, for Isis had kept the child hidden in the swamps

24

*Isis and Osiris.*
*From* Book of the Dead
*of Hunefer.* British Museum

throughout his boyhood. When the two men met, a ferocious battle took place. In the course of the fight, Horus hacked off his uncle's testicles, and Seth tore out Horus' eye. The bloody quarrel between Seth and Horus was presented for judgment to the earth-god, Geb, who recognized Horus as the successor to his father's throne. Later Horus became god of the sky and was represented as a hawk.

Horus performed the Opening of the Mouth ceremony for his murdered father, Osiris. For countless generations afterward, Egyptians had repeated the ceremony, endlessly restoring the sacred relationship between the living and the dead. Now Ramose was continuing this tradition. He set platters of food on a low altar for Meritptah's spirit to "feed" on. They were piled high with choice fruits and vegetables, bread, pastry, meat, beer, wine and other food and drink. Ramose also brought offerings of clothing and perfume, things which his wife had enjoyed in her lifetime, so that all the pleasures of Meritptah's life could be enjoyed in the world beyond.

Ancient Egyptians believed that everyone had a *ba* and a *ka*, which were parts of a person's personality, separate from the body. The *ba* was the soul, which resided within the body. At the moment of death, the *ba* would fly away from the deceased and take its place in the boat of the sun-god. The *ba* would journey around the earth in the sun-god's boat during the day. If the body was preserved, the *ba* would return to it and maintain contact between the dead person's body and the living world. The *ba* was represented as a bird with a human head resembling that of the deceased. The *ka* was the invisible

*Ba bird. From mummy of Tutankhamun.* The Metropolitan Museum of Art, photograph by Harry Burton

twin, which was born with the person and stayed with him or her throughout life. After death, the *ka* resided in the tomb, in a statue of the deceased.

Ramose brought food to Meritptah's tomb because her *ka* had to be cared for; otherwise it might wander away to look for something to eat and not return.

When all of the offerings had been placed on the altar, Ramose set the statue of his dead wife back in its niche. He bowed low, silently, straightening himself up with painful slowness. Walking backward, he left the chamber, sweeping away all the marks of his footsteps in the dust with a palm leaf.

27

# 5 In the Tomb

The morning ceremonies were finished, and now Ramose could devote the rest of the day to checking on the progress of the construction of his tomb. Ramose's old friend Per-Nefer, Master of Works, chief craftsman and cupbearer to Amenhotep IV, had supervised the early years of construction and decoration. Ramose, like other viziers of Egypt, knew the fundamentals of architecture. So when Per-Nefer was chosen to go to the new capital of the young Pharaoh Akhenaten, the vizier decided to finish the building of his tomb himself. Two other old friends, who remained in Thebes, the sculptor Men and the painter Bek, advised him on the work of the craftsmen.

When Ramose had begun constructing his underground burial place, the young Pharaoh Amenhotep IV had not yet forsaken the Theban god Amun for the sun-god Aten. Most of the decorations in Ramose's tomb were in the traditional style. Dignified figures were carefully carved in delicate relief. Ramose went through the inner chamber into the main hall. On one side of the doorway Amenhotep IV is portrayed in the traditional style, seated on a throne with Ramose paying homage to him. Servants bearing fans attend the Pharaoh, and courtiers bend down before him. Ramose sighed as he gazed at the sight of himself bowing to the Pharaoh. He turned away and his eyes shifted to the later relief on the other side of the doorway. There he had ordered his sculptors to carve the figure

*Courtiers and servants. From Tomb of Ramose.* Photograph courtesy of The Metropolitan Museum of Art

*Akhenaten and Nefertiti at window of appearances. Mutilated relief from Tomb of Ramose.* Photograph courtesy of The Metropolitan Museum of Art

of Akhenaten in the new, soft style which the young Pharaoh admired. Akhenaten and Nefertiti are portrayed in a realistic manner, with thick lips and rounded belly. He and his queen are standing at the window of appearances in their palace, where they appeared in public. Overhead the sun-god is shown as a heavenly disk with numerous rays radiating outward, each ending in a tiny human hand, some of which are holding an *ankh*, the symbol of life. Ramose is portrayed receiving the gold chain of office from the king.

The vizier could not surpress the surge of anger that arose within him. How high his hopes had been that he could retain the favor of Akhenaten. How sad he felt for his vanished dreams.

Ramose's tomb had more than five hundred square yards of wall space for decoration. Much of this space was being used to preserve the memory of the nobleman himself and his family, especially his parents and his wife's parents, and to show his accomplishments in office.

Continuing his inspection, the vizier walked along the north wall of the main hall. A handsome portrait of Ramose was carved in relief and his name and titles were inscribed in hieroglyphs. As he walked along, his eyes caught some of the listings describing him: "Beloved of the Pharaoh, Special Companion, Chancellor of the North, Vizier, Superintendent of Documents, Superintendent of Great Monuments, Judge, Priest of Justice." There were many others. His father's name, Neby, was also inscribed, along with his titles, as were his brother's name and titles.

Ancient Egyptians believed that a person's name had to be legible forever. It was feared that if after death the person's name was obliterated, his or her memory would fade in the land of the living. "Let my name abide in your house" went an inscription on an old Egyptian monument. "Let my *ka* be remembered after my life. Let my statue abide and my name endure upon it imperishably in your temple." Also carved on the north wall were servants bringing offerings of fruit, fowl and flowers.

Ramose went over to watch some of the workmen. The stonemasons were having problems. The rough walls of the tomb were irregular and often needed smoothing to provide a flat surface for the draftsmen, who sketched the outlines for the sculptors to follow. These draftsmen were superb craftsmen, skillful and sure. Ramose was pleased with the work done so far. Pictures of him and his relatives had been sketched on the walls, but much of the carving was still to be finished.

Ramose admired the carvings on the east wall showing his relatives at a banquet. Included were his father and mother, Neby and Yupuya, and his brother Amenhotep and his wife

*Neby and Yupuya, father and mother of Ramose. From Tomb of Ramose.* Photograph courtesy of The Metropolitan Museum of Art

Mayet. The faces of the men and women were superbly carved in the traditional manner. All are wearing elaborate wigs. One of the figures on the wall represents Ramose carrying the symbols of his rank and wearing the great gold chain of his office.

Some of the sculptors argued about the need for delicate modeling in the relief carving. Why bother with fine carving when it was too dark in the tomb for it to be seen? The sculptors, who were called "the enliveners," were particularly troubled by Ramose's insistence that the eyes be modeled with care. Carved lines were delicate, they agreed, but in the darkness of the tomb the subtle modeling of the eyes would hardly be noticeable. The painters added that it might be helpful to outline the eyes with dark paint; otherwise they would seem empty and blind. Ramose listened, but he remained steadfast in his decision: There was to be no paint to mar the lines of the heads and eyes. Ramose believed that the dead, not the living, would be looking at the relief carving in his tomb, and that they would appreciate the delicate work.

The workmen sighed as they heard Ramose's orders, and they returned to their tasks. It would take a long time to finish the fine-line wall carvings that Ramose was insisting upon.

The vizier paused for a minute before the unfinished paintings on the south wall, and he was overwhelmed with sadness. One scene showed his dead wife leading a group of wailing women behind a coffin. Ramose had been certain that his lovely young wife would outlive him. So the picture showed her with her arms raised in a gesture of grief for him. An attendant

Meritptah and mourning women. From Tomb of Ramose. Photograph courtesy of The Metropolitan Museum of Art

supports Meritptah. The artists tried to make the figures of her and the mourning women lifelike. The women's garments are loose and flowing and their breasts are bare. Among them is a child too young to be clothed. Tears pour down their cheeks, and some throw dust on their heads, in mourning. The servants bearing offerings are stiff, in the traditional manner of Egyptian art. Their bodies are shown in profile, while their shoulders and eyes are represented as if seen from the front. Sadly

Servants bearing offerings. From Tomb of Ramose.
Photograph courtesy of The Metropolitan Museum of Art

Ramose thought of how fate had fooled him and Meritptah had died first. Ramose urged the men to work faster, so the tomb could be completed.

The aging vizier walked slowly down to Meritptah's burial chamber. The stone sarcophagus of Meritptah lay in a sunken room, 55 feet below the ground level of the tomb. Alongside the sarcophagus of his wife was another one which Ramose had reserved for himself. He stood looking at his wife's sarcophagus and wondered when he would be joining her.

When Ramose returned to the great hall he called for his metalworkers and jewelers, who had come to the tomb to meet with him. These craftsmen were making beautiful vessels for the tomb and precious jewelry that would be buried with Ramose's mummy. Many of the metal objects they were making were copper, which came from mines in the hills and desert of Sinai, and from southern Nubia.

He was pleased with the copper objects and the necklaces and bracelets made of gold set with semiprecious stones. But he also wanted a statuette of pure gold to put into his tomb, as the Pharaohs did. Most of the gold came to Egypt as tribute from Nubia, which was under Egyptian rule. Gold was prized for its beauty, and its gleam rivaling that of the sun. This metal is everlasting, as it neither rusts nor decays.

Silver was more scarce than gold at this time, and was considered very valuable. The natural combination of silver and gold, called electrum or "white gold," was especially prized.

Ramose also conferred with the craftsman who was making tiny figurines in the form of mummies with hands crossed over the chest, holding farm implements. These statuettes are called *shawabtis* . . . the "answerers," because it was thought they could be summoned by the dead master to do his work for him, especially to tend the vegetable gardens in the afterworld.

Ramose had painted on the walls of his tomb the usual instructions to the shawabtis: "Oh Shawabti, if the name of Osiris Ramose [meaning "Ramose has died, been mummified, and joined Osiris"] is called for work in the Heavenly Fields for such tasks as tilling the soil or carting sand, speak up for him in his place and shout: 'Look! Here I am! I am doing it!' "

*Ushabti.*
Courtesy of The Brooklyn Museum,
Charles Edwin Wilbour Fund

Ramose took the time to talk to the woodworkers. Wood was considered precious, and woodworking was a rare skill. There were no trees in the Nile River valley, as trees could not grow in the desert land, but various kinds of woods were imported from abroad—cedar, cypress, ebony, juniper, fir, yew and oak. Ramose's woodworkers had already built him a boat to cruise on the Nile. Now they were going to make elaborate coffins for him.

The day had been long. Ramose felt weary. He was eager to get home and rest before sunset, when his cook would have a tasty meal for him, which he planned to share with some old friends.

# 6 The Evening of Ramose's Last Day

The ride back through the streets of Thebes in his litter seemed longer than usual to Ramose. He reached his palace just as the sun was setting below the rim of the western desert.

A servant met him at the door and took off his master's wig, which was made of human hair and beeswax. The cool air felt refreshing on his scalp. The servant also took the white linen robe Ramose had been wearing all day. In his chamber, Ramose put on a fresh robe. He wore only linen, made from flax that grew in the Nile Valley. Linen is cool. Cotton and silk were not yet known in Egypt. Wool was considered ritually unclean.

Ramose's spirits rose as his guests arrived. That night, dinner was exceptionally elaborate. There were dishes of beef, lamb and goat meat as well as wild geese from the marshes along the Nile. No pork dishes were included, because the flesh of the pig was considered unclean. Fish was not served either. Many varieties could be caught in the Nile, but without ice it did not keep well. Fish was popular in the diet of the poor, who would consume their catch without delay.

In addition to the main courses of meat and fowl, the meal included a variety of vegetables . . . onions, leeks, beans, peas, lentils, pumpkins, spinach and radishes. Salt, which came from the Delta, was used for seasoning. There was bread, which had been baked on heated stones. Also included was an assortment

*Making wine and preparing food. Wall painting from Tomb of Nakht*

of fruits: figs, dates, grapes, pomegranates and berries. And to slake dry throats, the servants poured beer and wine.

The guests sat on low chairs made of wood; some were folding chairs with leather seats. A low, portable table was set before each person. The food was served in simple bowls. There were no knives and forks, so the diners picked up the food with their fingers. Each guest was given a lotus flower to

38

smell, and a bowl for wine or beer. Servants stood by with whisks to brush away the flies. And all during dinner musicians played softly, on a lute, a double flute and a harp. Beautiful girls performed dances for the entertainment of Ramose and his guests.

Ramose ate without much appetite, but his guests enjoyed the meal enormously. Over dinner they talked of the changes which were taking place all around them. Would the strange cult of the sun, so dear to the heart of the new Pharaoh Akhenaten, survive after his death? They also discussed the priests of Amun at Thebes, who were furious at Akhenaten for driving them out of power by changing Egypt's religion. But it was certain that they would not give up easily. The new city of Akhetaten had been built quickly, and it could be destroyed just as quickly.

*Musicians. Wall painting from Tomb of Nakht*

The guests also wondered who would follow Akhenaten to the throne, since he had five daughters but no sons. What did they think of the birth of a new prince named Tutankhaten? He was a brother of the Pharaoh and might become the next ruler, if he should marry one of Akhenaten's daughters. But he might not live long enough, for the child was reported to have a frail constitution. The priests of Thebes would, in any case, have to agree to support him for the royal succession. If they did, the dinner guests commented, they would probably make him change his name to Tutankhamun.

What about Queen Nefertiti's father, Ay, as a possible successor? An impressive figure—he was taller than the average Egyptian—Ay was the King's Lieutenant of Chariotry and Master of the Horse, as his father Yuya had been before him. If no legitimate heir was available and Ay took over the throne, what kind of ruler would he make?

The moon was high in the heavens when Ramose's friends sipped their last glass of wine and said good night. As the voices of his guests trailed off, the house seemed lonely to Ramose. Quietly the servants went about, preparing their master's bed.

As was his custom before bedtime, Ramose climbed to the roof of his palace to look at the stars. The palace, built of sun-dried mud brick, was three stories high. The roof afforded a view of the Nile on one side and the desert on the other. He called for a servant to bring him a couch, and he stretched out, letting his thoughts wander up to the jeweled sky. Beyond the Nile, Ramose could see the black shadows of the mountains which were thought to separate the land of the dead from the

*Tutankhamun.*
The Metropolitan Museum of Art,
photograph by Harry Burton

land of the living. Egyptians believed the dead lived exactly as they had during their lifetimes, in a land that ran parallel to the Nile and partly beneath it.

Ramose's thoughts continued to wander as he lay on his couch under the stars. He felt his strength ebbing, but he was not in pain. His breathing began to falter, becoming slower and deeper. Unknown to him, he was on his way to rejoin his wife and parents.

Like other Egyptians, Ramose expected on his death to pass through the dark Underworld in a boat. He would go through a gloomy underground region that was haunted by fearful fiends and monsters. In this dread region, anyone whose faith

41

*Agricultural activities in the Heavenly Fields. Wall painting from Tomb of Sennodem.* The Metropolitan Museum of Art, photograph by Egyptian Expedition

was weak would be seized and tortured, and then burned up and devoured. But hopefully, Ramose would eventually reach the blessed land of Osiris. Sailing underneath the cities of Egypt, he would pass through a succession of gates which would open when he gave the right password. At the end of the journey, he would reach the Heavenly Fields, in the western corner of the Underworld. The Heavenly Fields were a land of eternal spring, ruled by Osiris, where all the pleasures of Ramose's lifetime would be waiting for him.

But before he could enter the Heavenly Fields, he would have to undergo the traditional Judgment of the Dead, a ceremony in which his heart would be weighed. According to ancient Egyptian belief, the heart was the seat of all intellect and emotion. The weighing-of-the-heart ceremony took place in the Hall of Maat, goddess of justice and truth. Osiris watched from his throne, wrapped in layers of linen, like a mummy. In the middle of the hall stood a large pair of scales of equal balance. The heart of the dead man was placed on one pan of the scales; on the other, an ostrich feather of the goddess Maat, the symbol of truth. The balance was then adjusted by the jackal-headed Anubis, who was in charge of the scales. The ibis-headed god Thoth, scribe of the gods, who had invented writing, mathematics and language, stood by to jot down the result of the weighing. Thoth's baboon sat on top of the scales. The dead man being judged would stand nervously, imploring the heart to be faithful and not inform against him. If the feather proved to be lighter than the heart, this meant that the man's bad deeds outweighed his good deeds. He would then be immediately thrown to Ammit, a fierce monster

*Ceremony of weighing the heart. From* Book of the Dead *of Ani.*
British Museum

who waited by the side of the balance, eager to tear the deceased to shreds. Ammit had the head of a crocodile, the forepaws of a lion, and the hindquarters of a hippopotamus. If the heart and the feather balanced, Anubis would announce to Osiris: "His heart is righteous." This meant the deceased was worthy of immortality. Horus would take him by the hand and lead him to Osiris' throne. Waiting for him would be the boat of the sun-god, which would take him to the kingdom of Osiris for a life of eternal happiness. Ramose believed, like all Egyptians, that once in the blessed fields of the kingdom of Osiris, he would be reunited with his wife and parents.

Now, as the early fall moon rose high in the heavens over Thebes, its silver light glowing on the roof of Ramose's house, he dozed off. Below, the city of Thebes lay in silent darkness. Now and then the mournful sign of a howling dog broke the stillness. Then Ramose's *ba* silently left his body and soared beyond the stars. Ramose was dead.

# 7 Death on the Roof

All the while that Ramose was on the roof, a young scribe, called Khnumbaf, had been downstairs in the house, busily writing on a long scroll of papyrus. Scribes sat cross-legged and wrote with reed pens. Paper made from the tall papyrus plants that grow in the marshes of the Nile was invented by the Egyptians. Strips of this plant were laid close together, edge to edge; other strips were laid across at right angles; then the strips were moistened with water, pressed, then pounded and allowed to dry, forming sheets of papyrus, which was the world's first paper. The sheets were pasted together to make rolls, or scrolls.

Khnumbaf was working on the *Book of the Coming Forth by Day*, which we call the *Book of the Dead*. He carefully copied down spells to help Ramose gain entrance to the next world, as well as magic formulas to preserve his spirit from danger. The spells were designed also to provide the vizier, when he died, with material needs and give him the power to enter and leave his tomb freely. The long scroll of papyrus was being prepared to be placed in Ramose's tomb. An artist was illustrating the text with pictures of the gods, the nobleman and his wife and family. Ready-made scrolls which had blank spaces to be filled in with the names of the departed could be brought from the undertaker. But kings and noblemen usually had a *Book of the Dead* individually written.

*Scribe.* The Brooklyn Museum, Charles Edwin Wilbour Fund

Khnumbaf prided himself on the artistry of his picture writing. He kept his reed pens clean, ready for use with the cakes of ink. His papyrus scrolls were neatly stacked. Carefully he worked over the *Book of the Dead*, brushing in the text in hieratic symbols. Hieratic is a cursive form of ancient Egyptian hieroglyphic writing.

The lamps flickered low as he worked over the long roll of papyrus. One wick sputtered in its dish of oil and died with a whisper. It was time to take a brief rest on the roof, which was pleasantly cool at night.

Silently he climbed the staircase to the roof. He took a few steps and stopped suddenly, fearful. There, stretched out on his couch, alone and unattended, lay Ramose. Would the young scribe be punished for disturbing the peaceful rest of his master?

Something about the prone figure of Ramose struck Khnumbaf as peculiar. Was the master really asleep? Khnumbaf tiptoed over to listen to the sound of the old man's breathing. There was no sign of breath. He bent over Ramose to listen to the beat of his heart. He could detect no sound.

The young man ran down the stairs and found the chief servant, who sent someone to summon a doctor. The doctor who rushed to the side of Ramose was one of the many specialists who practiced medicine in Thebes. He was primarily a stomach specialist. Others dealt with head complaints, female disorders, teeth, eyes and even beauty treatments. The doctor bent over Ramose and listened for the sound of his breathing and his heart, and felt for his pulse, but Ramose was dead. Had

Ramose been alive, the doctor would have recited spells as he moved the vizier's arms and legs. He would have ordered potions, made of women's milk mixed with oil and salt, for the patient to swallow. It seemed to the doctor that Ramose had died of internal causes. The doctor stood motionless for a moment, and sighed at the loss of an old friend.

# 8 Mummification and Funeral Rites

At dawn, a steward was sent to the Per-Nefer, or "Beautiful House," also called the "House of Purification," to fetch Amasis the priest, who would arrange for Ramose's mummification and funeral. Amasis hurried to Ramose's palace, accompanied by his assistants. When they reached the dead man, they solemnly recited formulas over the silent figure before lifting him up and carrying him away.

Years earlier, the vizier and the priest Amasis had discussed the details of Ramose's mummification and funeral. They had agreed that a man of his exalted position should have the most expensive mummifying procedure, which took a full ten weeks. There were cheaper methods, but these were for lower-class Egyptians who could not afford to pay for the best.

Amasis sent for the chief mason of Ramose's tomb and told him that he must complete all work in seventy days. He instructed the artists and sculptors to lose no time finishing the decorations. A few additional suggestions were made about the carved figures on the walls. With so little time left to finish all of the carving, the "enliveners" felt they could disregard Ramose's order and use paint to finish the eyes. Also, other wall decorations that had started as carvings would have to be finished with paint. The craftsmen hurried back to the west bank of the Nile to their tasks. Amasis then called in the young

*Craftsmen making funerary objects. Wall painting
from Tomb of Nebamun and Ipuky*

scribe Khnumbaf and looked over the progress of the *Book of
the Dead.* He, too, was given instructions to complete his work
within seventy days.

Amasis also spoke to the women of Ramose's household and
reminded them of their duties: They were to appear in public
grief-stricken and mournful. The professional mourners, hired
for the occasion, were sent wandering through the streets of
Thebes, singing sad songs about the shortness of life and the
virtues of the dead man, and shrieking and throwing dust on
their heads. Friends of the dead man were asked to abstain
from wine for the period of mourning and to avoid any lavish
display of dress.

By the time the priest Amasis had finished the preliminary
arrangements, Ramose's body had reached the Beautiful

House, where his remains would be purified and mummified. The practice of mummification had taken centuries to reach its current stage of perfection, and the secrets of the trade were guarded preciously. Every embalmer knew human anatomy in complete detail.

The embalming process was carried out according to a definite ritual. Priests recited spells as each step was completed. The priests and their assistants had to prepare the dead man so that his *ba* and his *ka*—his soul and his twin spirit—could recognize his face. Preserving the features so that a man's face could be identified required skill. During the prolonged rites of mummification, one of the embalmers wore a jackal-headed mask to impersonate the god Anubis, who had mummified Osiris.

Ramose's body was stripped of the clothes he had been

*Anubis performing mummification. Wall painting from Tomb of Sennodem.* The Metropolitan Museum of Art, photograph by Egyptian Expedition

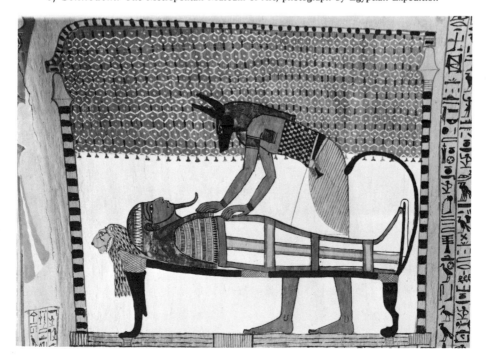

wearing when he died. Carefully the embalmers washed his face, his body, his arms and legs; then gently they laid him on a long table. The process of preserving his body for eternity had begun.

An assistant embalmer named Weni picked up a special chisel-like tool and carefully inserted it into the skull cavity of the dead man. One end of the tool was hooked; Weni skillfully severed the brain tissue from the skull and cut the soft matter into many pieces. The brain tissue had to be removed without delay because it decays quickly. Using another rod, which was bent along the inner edge, Weni pulled out the bits of brain matter through the nostrils.

Hesira, another assistant, who was a scribe, traced a line with special ink on the left flank of Ramose's body, leading up from the groin. A third assistant, Nebenmaat, would make an incision along the line Hesira had drawn on the skin.

Nebenmaat, who was called "the cutter," picked up a sharp stone knife. It was his duty to cut open the body, a step absolutely necessary for the embalming process, but offensive nevertheless to Egyptians, who wanted the body to be intact and unblemished. Nebenmaat often found himself alone and shunned by the other embalmers, as it was part of the ceremony to make the cutter an outcast.

With his sharp knife, called an Ethiopian stone, Nebenmaat made a deep cut, following the line of ink drawn on the body. As soon as he had finished, all the other assistants pelted him with stones and drove him out of the mummifying room, cursing him for defiling the body. It was a symbolic act, per-

formed as a ritual time and
again, for as Porphyry wrote in
the third century A.D., "Whoso-
ever inflicts violence upon, or
wounds, or in any way injures a
body of his kind, they [the Egyp-
tians] hold worthy of hatred."

Now Amasis' other assistants
went to work on Ramose's body.
One of them removed the viscera, or internal organs. First the
stomach, liver and intestines
were removed, then the kidneys.
The next step was to cut the diaphragm and take out the lungs.

Amasis reminded his assistant
that the heart of the dead
Ramose should be specially
taken care of. Carefully one of
the embalmers removed the
heart from Ramose's body. It
was embalmed and put into a
special jar. Ramose's heart was
replaced by a scarab, a carved
stone in the shape of a beetle.
The scarab beetle represented
eternal life to the ancient Egyp-

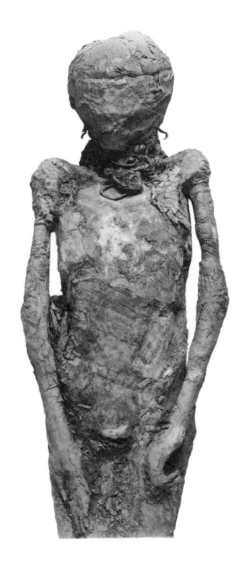

*Mummy of Queen Merytamun showing incision.*
*Jewelry marks on head, arms and chest can also be seen.*
The Metropolitan Museum of Art, photograph by Egyptian Expedition

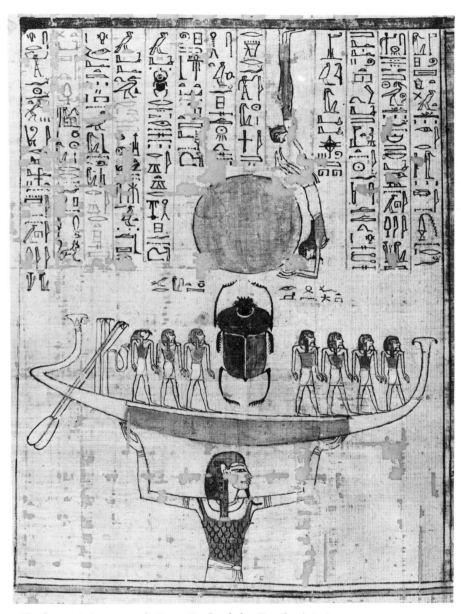

*The boat of the sun-god. From* Book of the Dead *of Ani.*
British Museum

tians. They considered this tiny insect to be hardworking, patient and strong. The beetle lays its eggs in a ball of dung, which it tirelessly rolls along on the ground. To the ancient Egyptians, this was like the sun-god, who pushed the sun, the source of all life, across the sky each day. The Egyptians represented the sun emerging from the eastern mountains every morning and being pushed by a beetle across the heavens in a boat that is held up by the sky.

The heart scarab placed in Ramose's body was inscribed on the bottom with these words in hieroglyphs:

My heart of my mother, my heart of my mother, my heart of my being, stand not up against me at my testifying; tender no evidence against me at my judgment. Be fair for us, make fair hearing at the weighing of the words. Speak not lies against me in front of the Great God. Surely you will be lifted up living.

The embalming process continued. To be preserved, the viscera, as well as the body, had to be dehydrated, or dried out. The internal organs and lungs from Ramose's body were carefully washed with palm wine and spices to sterilize them. Then they were put on a small, slanting bed and covered with a chemical substance called natron, which is a mixture of sodium carbonate and sodium bicarbonate, combined with sodium chloride, which is common salt, or sodium sulphate. This chemical mixture could be found in several places in Egypt where water, in which the sodium compounds were dissolved, bubbled to the surface and evaporated, leaving behind a deposit of the natron.

The internal organs and lungs were left in the natron for forty days. At the end of this time they were sterilized once more with spices and rubbed with perfumed oil and sweet-smelling resin. The lungs, liver, intestines and stomach were each carefully wrapped like a mummy in long strips of linen, on which were inscribed the names of the four sons of Horus, the genies of the dead, who were in charge of protecting the viscera: the human-headed Imsety guarded the liver; the ape-headed Hapi protected the lungs: Duamutef, the jackal-headed son, looked after the stomach; and the hawk-headed Kebekh-senuef protected the intestines. A tiny mummy mask was placed at the top of each of these miniature mummified viscera. The mask was made of cartonnage, layers of coarse linen glued together and coated with plaster, and covered with gold. When these had been placed inside the four canopic jars, they were set in a chest which was mounted on a sledge, a low wooden cart on wide runners. The chest was inscribed with prayers to the goddess Nut to spread her protective wings over the deceased.

Now the chest cavity and the stomach regions were washed with palm wine and spices, then stuffed with linen packets of natron to speed the drying out of the body tissues. The body was also stuffed with linen bags of sweet-smelling gums and resins to counteract any odor that might develop. Care was taken to coat the internal cavity completely, thus killing any bacteria and forming an airtight seal to preserve the soft tissue.

Carefully and gently, the embalmers picked up Ramose's body and set it in a mound of natron on a slanting board called

*Mummified viscera and canopic jar.*
From *The Tomb of Iouiya and Touiyou*
by Thoedore M. Davis et al, London, 1907

the bed of mummification, where it would remain for forty days. At the lower end of the slanted bed was a small canal leading to a basin, in which the water extracted from the body was collected.

During this time, Ramose's friends observed the rites of mourning. And the chief stonemason, the sculptor, and the painter were wasting no time in getting his tomb, or "House of Eternity," ready for him.

At the end of forty days, the dehydration or drying-out process was finished. The body was removed from its natron bed, carefully sponged and dried. By now, Ramose's skin was clinging to his bones. His flesh had shrunk, but the hair was well preserved, and his hands and feet still had nails: They had been tied on to his fingers and toes. His face was drawn and thin, but had changed little otherwise.

*Mummy of Yuya.* From *The Tomb of Iouiya and Touiyou* by Theodore M. Davis et al, London, 1907

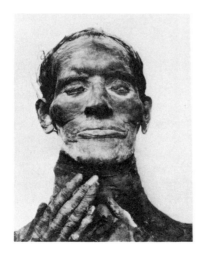

Amasis watched as his helpers removed the packets of natron which had been used as temporary stuffing in the chest and abdominal cavities. This stuffing and everything that had touched the body during the embalming process was carefully gathered together. These things were packed into large pots, to be buried safely near the tomb of the deceased, to protect him from enemies who might try to bewitch him by possessing a part of him.

Now the time had come to pack the body cavities. Linen soaked with resin and spices was stuffed into the skull through the nostrils, which were then plugged with beeswax. The chest was packed with linen bags filled with fresh, dry natron and the spices myrrh and cinnamon. Other linen packets were soaked with resin and packed with sawdust and an onion.

When it was time to close the incision, the chief priest again appeared to examine the body of his old friend. As he looked on, the embalming incision was drawn together and closed with a paste of resin and beeswax. The incision was sewn together with fine linen thread. Since Ramose had been an important nobleman, a small plate of gold, inscribed with the sacred eye of Horus, was put over the cut in his body. The eye indicated that Horus watched over Ramose's body as he did over the body of his father Osiris.

Ramose's whole body was rubbed with cedar oil and other fragrant ointments. His mouth was packed with linen and wax. His eyeballs were pressed down and covered with linen pads soaked in resin, and the eyelids were drawn down. Every effort was made to have his eyes appear as they had when Ramose was still alive. To reduce the brittleness of the skin and keep it from being dampened by any moisture, the whole body surface was smeared with melted resin.

Now his legs were brought close together, and his arms were laid over his chest, with one wrist crossing the other. The nails of his hands were stained with henna, and rings inscribed with the dead man's name and titles were placed on the little finger of his left hand. A gold cap was placed over each finger and toe, to protect it from being crushed. Then a heart scarab, made of fine green stone and encased in gold, was hung on a gold chain around the neck of the deceased. A girdle of round beads, with a hawk pendant, was wound around Ramose's abdomen, and a broad collar made of gold and inlaid with semiprecious stones was laid over his breast. Bracelets and anklets were placed on his arms and legs, and gold sandals on his feet.

Amasis called in his bandagers. These skillful workmen had been preparing long strips of linen. The strips were about three inches wide; one edge was gummed. At the ends of the strips, Ramose's name had been written so that there would be no mistake in identifying the mummy.

With delicate care, the embalmers wrapped separate bandages around each finger and toe, then around the hands, arms and feet. Thick pads of linen were laid over the feet to prevent any injury when the coffin was set on end and the mummy made to stand upright for the Opening of the Mouth ceremony. Starting at the feet, more bandages were wrapped around the limbs and body, layer upon layer. Folds of linen

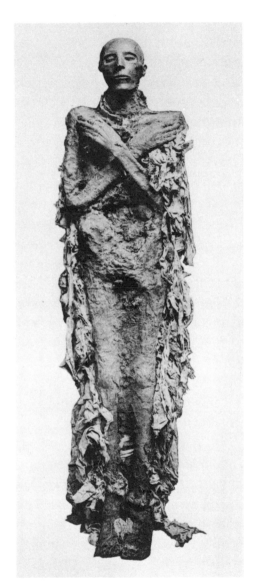

*Unwrapped mummy of Seti I with arms crossed.* Cairo Museum

*Unwrapped mummy of Tutankhamun with collars and amulets on his neck.* Courtesy of The Metropolitan Museum of Art, photograph by Harry Burton

were then laid horizontally across the body. Other wrappings were set perpendicularly. The body had lost its outward shape under more than twenty layers of wrapping.

A band of linen stretching down from head to toe and back again held the head in position. Four bandages of orange-colored linen were wrapped around the shoulders, the middle, the knees and the ankles. All together, several hundred yards of linen were used. Some of it was old household linen that the family had been saving for this occasion. Linen straps were fastened over the wrappings. Scarabs and other amulets were laid over various parts of the body. Garlands of fresh flowers were placed around the neck and on the head. Ramose's mummy was complete.

Seventy days had passed since Ramose had died on the roof of his palace overlooking the Nile. Now the preparations were concluded and the day had come when a mummy mask would be put on Ramose's face and he would be gently put into the mummy cases, or coffins. Ramose's few old friends stood by silently, remembering.

During the seventy days while the body of Ramose was being mummified, the carpenters and artists had been busy in the "House of Purification," finishing the coffins for the final entombment. The carpenters had taken careful measurements of the body before it was embalmed and made allowance for the extra space that would be taken up by the thick layers of bandages, for the mummy had to fit into the inner coffin exactly. This inner coffin was made of sycamore planks, two inches thick. The sections were fitted together with wooden pegs.

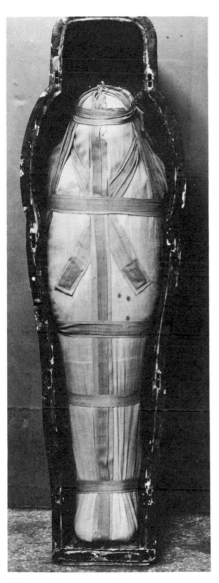

*Wrapped mummy of a queen
of Dynasty 21.* British Museum

*Wrapped mummy of a priestess
of Dynasty 22 with
wooden mask and amulets.*
British Museum

An artist had made sketches of Ramose's face. A likeness was modeled into a cartonnage mask that was fitted over the face of the mummy. The eyes and eyebrows of the mask were inlaid with colored glass.

Three separate wooden, mummiform coffins that would fit closely one inside the other had been made for Ramose. The nobleman's mummy was carefully laid inside the first coffin, which was covered with stucco, or fine plaster, and gold, and inlaid with semiprecious stones and colored glass. A pectoral, or necklace, was carved over the neck on the cover of the mummy case, and over the abdomen was a carving of the

*Cartonnage mummy mask.* From *The Tomb of Iouiya and Touiyou* by Theodore M. Davis et al, London, 1907

vulture goddess, with her wings outspread. Below it, between columns of hieroglyphs, stood a figure of Nut, with her arms upraised.

Now the innermost coffin was set into the second mummy case, which was covered with silver and gold, and inlaid with colored glass. Carved over the chest were hands, which were crossed, as the mummy's hands had been crossed. The third, or outer coffin, was covered with black pitch.

Now the lid of the outer coffin was firmly secured and it was put into a model boat with oars and placed on a sledge. The boat signified a mythical journey down the Nile River to the sacred city of Abydos, where the gap existed through which the soul could pass directly into the afterworld. Ramose was ready for his long journey to eternity.

*Innermost coffin.*
From *The Tomb of Iouiya and Touiyou*
by Theodore M. Davis et al, London, 1907

The day of Ramose's funeral had been set by his few relatives and friends. Into his house had come all the furniture, urns and jewelry which would accompany him to his tomb. Now Ramose came home one last time.

Amasis and his assistants had arranged an elaborate procession for Ramose's funeral. Everyone was given a place. Professional mourners had been hired, who beat their bare breasts, poured dust on their heads and clothes, and went through the motions of pulling out their hair, while wailing loudly. Streams of tears poured from every eye. The priests, burning incense and reciting prayers, walked in the procession through the streets of Thebes. Two women impersonated the goddesses Isis and Nephthys. They were followed by a long line of servants carrying objects to be placed in the tomb, including offerings to the gods and all the objects Ramose might need in his afterlife, and servants also carried offering tables with food, such as bread, cakes, ducks, haunches of beef, and vegetables. Other men marched with flowers and jars containing wine, beer, oil and perfume, chests of clothes and jewels and vases for libations, or offerings to the gods. A bearer groaned under the weight of a funerary bed; another carried a chair, and another a light stool. Objects that Ramose had used in his lifetime came next: his sandals, his scribe's palette, along with a box of brushes and other instruments for writing and drawing, a fan, a walking stick and a harp that he had enjoyed playing in his leisure.

One marcher carried a board on which were written

66

*Offering bearers. Wall painting from Tomb of Ramose.*
Photograph courtesy of The Metropolitan Museum of Art

Ramose's names and titles, together with prayers to the gods of the underworld. A sledge was loaded with the coffer which held the four canopic jars containing Ramose's embalmed internal organs.

Other bearers were laden with the tiny shawabti figures which would be set in the tomb with Ramose. Men carried long poles on their shoulders, from which were suspended boxes of flowers. A group of women followed, some with their breasts bared, their hair disheveled. Among the wailing women were Ramose's female servants, who showed genuine grief at losing a comfortable home and a good master.

On their way to the Nile, the funeral procession passed through narrow streets crowded with people, who turned to admire the magnificent coffin as it was dragged by slowly on the sledge. A priest, wearing a panther skin and holding a bronze censer for burning incense, scattered holy water. Behind marched a number of other priests wearing white linen robes.

At the Nile, the solemn procession dissolved in confusion. The herds of animals to be sacrificed thrashed about wildly as they were loaded onto a boat. The scene was one of shouting,

*Wall painting of coffin on sledge. From Tomb of Paimy.*
The Metropolitan Museum of Art, photograph by Egyptian Expedition

rushing, pushing. The coffin and the tomb offerings were set in place. The mourners climbed aboard and the funeral boats pushed off.

On the west bank it took an hour to get everyone and everything unloaded, but finally the procession re-formed in the order in which it would proceed to the tomb. The cortege continued through green fields where farmers stopped their work to stare at the sight. Then it moved onward to the rugged valley in the western desert and passed along the cliffs where noble Egyptians had carved their tombs. Through the rocky gorges, it proceeded slowly over the rough ground. Farther on, the procession reached a rectangular opening in the side of a hill, where priests were waiting with a party of tomb guardians, attendants and workmen. Musicians and dancers were also waiting. They would perform for the guests at a banquet after the funeral.

The coffin was lifted out and carried to the entrance of the tomb. There it was raised upright by a priest wearing the jackal-headed mask of Anubis. Before the upright coffin, attendants set up tables and piled them high with offerings of flowers, wine and food. The herds of animals to be sacrificed were led to the tomb. While Ramose's mummy was standing upright, facing the crowd, priests performed the ceremony of the Opening of the Mouth. They were guided by a priest wearing a leopard-skin robe. The ritual was supposed to restore the senses, speech, and movement to the deceased, so that he might enjoy all of his daily activities in the afterlife. The mouth and eyes of the carved face on the coffin were anointed with oil and the lips touched by a hooked instrument, as though they were being parted. Then a priest spoke, repeating the rites that Horus had performed for his murdered father, Osiris: "You live again, you revive always, you have become young again, you are young again, and forever."

The moment of leave-taking came. The wailing women and the few distant relatives said farewell as the mummy in its

*Opening of the Mouth ceremony. From* Book of the Dead *of Hunefer.*
British Museum

coffin was taken to the slanting ramp leading down to the burial chamber and lowered deep into the ground to rest in a stone sarcophagus alongside Meritptah. The funerary offerings, the table, chairs, bed, jars, coffers and all the other gifts to the dead, were lowered into the tomb and set in place in the burial chamber. When the last person had left the tomb, masons sealed the doorway with slabs of stone, and the tomb entrance was hidden behind sand and rocks. The hope was that it could be kept secret from greedy grave robbers. Unfortunately, it was not.

# Postscript

Ramose's tomb was broken into and his mummy was carried off in ancient times, no one knows when. Along with the mummy went the precious possessions that were buried with him. In 1879, Ramose's tomb was discovered by the English archaeologist Villiers Stuart. It was partly restored by Sir Robert Mond in 1904, and by 1927 it was fully cleared of rubble. Now it is there for all to see when they visit Luxor; it is known as Number 55 of the Tombs of the Nobles. Almost all that we know about Ramose is from this tomb, especially its beautiful wall paintings, relief carvings and inscriptions.

We based our story of mummification in ancient Egypt on this particular nobleman because his tomb illustrates one of the most dramatic periods of Egyptian history. He lived during the time when Egypt was at the height of its power and dominated the ancient world. During this period, the Egyptian Empire extended from the Fourth Cataract of the Nile in Ethiopia in the south to the Euphrates River in Mesopotamia in the north. Egypt was the wealthiest and most powerful nation in the world. Rich tribute poured into the country from conquered lands, and caravans laden with Egyptian goods traveled throughout the ancient world.

Ramose was especially interesting to us because he served Amenhotep the Magnificent and his son Akhenaten. The latter Pharaoh is one of the most fascinating personalities in all Egyptian history, because he broke away from established tradition and formed his own religion. The decorations in Ramose's tomb, which are dated around 1370 B.C., depict both the old, classical style and Akhenaten's new style of art.

The exact dates of Ramose's birth and death are uncertain. However, we estimate that he was born around 1432 B.C. and lived about sixty years. It is thought that Amenhotep III reigned from about 1417 to 1367 and Akhenaten from about 1378 to 1362. Although there is much dispute among scholars in the matter, we believe that the father and son were co-regents for eleven years. We also believe that Ramose did not go to Tell el Amarna with Akhenaten, although scholars have differing opinions.

Late in Akhenaten's reign he had as his co-regent Smenkhkare, who was on the throne but a short time. At their deaths, Akhenaten's younger brother Tutankhaten ascended the throne. This young king moved back to Thebes, changing his name to Tutankhamun.

Our story is based on evidence from Egyptian history and on information from archaeological sources. However, we took the liberty of dramatizing the last day in the life of Ramose, based on what is known about life in general in the Eighteenth Dynasty. The Pharaohs and noblemen that we mention are historical figures. The names of the ordinary people are not known, so we chose names that were common in the period.

The photographs that we used to illustrate our story are the wall paintings and carvings in Ramose's tomb. And we used paintings from other Eighteenth and Nineteenth dynasty tombs in order to present a broad visual picture. Since Ramose's mummy was lost, we have taken the liberty of showing some of the few mummies which were not destroyed. Objects illustrated are from tombs that were not despoiled as Ramose's was. We based our description of Ramose's canopic jars, mummy mask and coffins on those found in the tomb of Tuya and Yuya, father and mother of Queen Teye, which was found almost intact in 1905 by the American archaeologist Theodore M. Davis.

There is no absolute consistency in the spelling of Egyptian names, since hieroglyphic writing did not indicate the vowels. The system used here is adopted from Sir Alan Gardiner's book *Egypt of the Pharaohs* (Oxford, 1961).

To research our story of Ramose we read dozens of books on Egyptian history, religion, daily life and art. We have chosen to list below only those books that directly relate to Ramose's tomb and to mummification practices.

The reader is reminded of co-author Shirley Glubok's books for young people that involve Egyptian art and archaeology: *The Art of Ancient Egypt* (Atheneum Publishers) and *Art and Archaeology* (Harper and Row, Publishers, Inc.). Her *Discovering Tut-Ankh-Amen's Tomb* (The Macmillan Company) should be especially interesting because its story of Egyptian mummies is told in reverse terms from *The Mummy of Ramose.* In the case of Tutankhamun, the archaeologists first discovered the tomb, then the coffins, and finally unwrapped the mummy.

We are grateful to a great many Egyptologists for their interest and advice: Robert Bianchi, Assistant Curator, Department of Egyptian and Classical Art, The Brooklyn Museum; Labib Habachi, former Chief Inspector of Upper Egypt, Department of Antiquities, Egypt; Christine Lilyquist, Curator of Egyptian Art, The Metropolitan Museum of Art; James Romano, Research Assistant, Department of Egyptian and Classical Art, The Brooklyn Museum; Pascal Vernus, French Institute of Archaeology, Cairo; Kent R. Weeks, Director, University of Chicago Epigraphic Survey, Luxor, Egypt.

Our special thanks go to Thomas J. Logan, Associate Curator of Egyptian Art, The Metropolitan Museum of Art, for his interest and friendship, and for giving us the benefit of his valuable advice.

# Selected Bibliography

Budge, Ernest A. Wallis. *The Mummy.* London, 1925, reprinted New York, Macmillan, 1972.

Davies, Norman de Garis. *The Tomb of the Vizier Ramose.* London, 1941.

Dawson, Warren. "Making a Mummy," *Journal of Egyptian Archaeology*, Vol. 13, 1927.

Edwards, I.E.S. *A Handbook to the Egyptian Mummies and Coffins Exhibited in the British Museum.* London, 1938.

Harris, James E., and Weeks, Kent R. *X-Raying the Pharaohs.* New York, 1972.

Herodotus. *The Histories*—there are many editions of the accounts of this fifth-century-B.C. Greek traveler in Egypt.

Iskander, Zaky. *A Brief History of Ancient Egypt.* Cairo, 1954.

Kamil, Jill. *Luxor: A Guide to Ancient Thebes.* London, 1973.

Lucas, A. *Ancient Egyptian Materials and Industries.* 4th edition, New York, 1962.

Martin, Richard A. *Mummies.* Chicago Natural History Museum, 1945.

Porter, Bertha, and Moss, Rosalind. *Topographical Bibliography of Ancient Egyptian Hieroglyphic Texts, Reliefs and Paintings.* Vol. I: *The Theban Necropolis*, Part I, "Private Tombs." Oxford, 1960.

Royal Ontario Museum. *Egyptian Mummies.* Toronto, 1950.

Sigerist, Henry A. *A History of Medicine.* Oxford, 1961.

Smith, G. Elliot. *The Royal Mummies.* Cairo, 1912.

Smith, G. Elliot, and Dawson, Warren. *Egyptian Mummies.* London, 1924.

OTHER SHIRLEY GLUBOK BOOKS ON RELATED SUBJECTS:

*The Art of Ancient Egypt* (Atheneum Publishers, 1962).

*Art and Archaeology* (Harper and Row, Publishers, Inc., 1966).

*Discovering Tut-Ankh-Amen's Tomb* (The Macmillan Company, 1968).

# Index

Page numbers in *italics* refer to illustrations.

Abdomen, 65
Abydos, 65
Agriculture, 16, *18*, 19, *42*. *See also* farmers, flax, harvest, linen, onions.
Akhenaten, 14, *14*, *29*, 30, 39, 40, 71, 72. *See also* Amenhotep IV.
Akhetaten, 13, 14, 39
Amasis (priest), 49, 50
Amenhotep (brother of Ramose), 31
Amenhotep III (Pharaoh), 4, 6, *7*, 8, 10, 15, 72; "Amenhotep the Magnificent," 8, 71
Amenhotep IV (Pharaoh), 10, 12, 14, *14*, 15, 28, 29, *29*
Amenhotep-Son-Of-Hapu (Vizier), 4, 9
Ammit (monster), 43, 44
Amulets, *61*, 62, *63*
Amun, 1, 6, 8, 10, 12, *13*, 28
Ani, *43*, *54*
Anubis, *51*, 43, 44, 51, 69
Aswan, 16
Ankh (symbol of life), 29
Arms, 60

Artists, 62. *See also* painters, sculptors.
Aten, 12, 13, 14, *14*, 28
Ay (Pharaoh), 12, 40

*Ba* (soul), 26, *27*, 44, 51
Bandages, 60, 62
Banquet, 69
Barley, 16. *See also* agriculture, food.
Beans, 16. *See also* agriculture, food.
"Beautiful House," 49, 50. *See also* "House of Purification."
Beef, 66. *See also* food.
Beer, 38, 39, 66
Beeswax, 59. *See also* resin, mummy.
Beetle, 53, 55. *See also* scarab.
Bek (painter), 28. *See also* painters.
Berries, 38
Boat, *2–3*, *54*, 65, 68
Bones, 58
Book of the Coming Forth by Day. *See* Book of the Dead.
Book of the Dead, *25*, *43*, 45, 47, 49, 50, *54*, *70*

Brain, 52. *See also* skull.
Bread, 37, 66. *See also* food.
Byblos, 23

Cakes, 66. *See also* food.
Canals. *See* irrigation.
Canopic jars, 56, *57*, 67, 73
Carpenters, 62
Cartonnage, 56, 64, *64*
Cataract, First, 16. *See also* Nile.
Cattle, 18
Ceremonies, *frontispiece, 43, 70.*
　*See also* "Judgment of the Dead,"
　"Mortuary Liturgy," "Opening of
　the Mouth," "Weighing of the
　Heart."
Chest (canopic), 56
Cinnamon, 59. *See also* spices.
Coffer, 23, 24
Coffin, 60, 62, 64, 65, *65*, 68, *68*,
　69, 70, 73. *See also* sarcophagus.
Collars, 34. *See also* jewels.
Cotton, 37
Co-regency, co-regent, 10, 12
Creation, miracle of, 17
Crook and flail, 24

Dancers, 69.
Dances, 39.
Dates, 38
Davis, Theodore M., 73
Delta, 16, 37. *See also* Nile.

Diaphragm, 53
Dikes. *See* irrigation
Dog Star. *See* Sirius.
Ducks, 66. *See also* fowl
Dynasties, 72, 73

Electrum (white gold), 34
Embalming, 51–53, 56–60, 62, 67.
　*See also* mummy, mummifica-
　tion, "House of Purification."
"Enliveners," 49. *See also* sculp-
　tors.
Ethiopia, 71
Ethiopian stone, 52
Euphrates River, 71
Eyes, 59, 64, 69

Face, 58, 64
Farmers, 16, *19, 42. See also* agri-
　culture.
Feet, 58, 60
Figs, 38
Fingers, 58, 60
Fish, 37. *See also* food.
Flail, crook and, 24
Flax, 16, 37. *See also* agriculture.
Flesh, 58
Flute, double, 39
Food, 37–38, *38*, 66, 69. *See also*
　barley, beans, onions.
Fowl, 37. *See also* food, ducks.
Fruits, 38. *See also* food.
Funeral, *frontispiece*, 49, 66, 68

Funerary furniture: bed, chair, stool, *19*, *27*, 66, 70

Geb (god), 26
Goat meat, 37. *See also* food.
Gold, 34, 56, 59, 60, 65
Grapes, 38
Grave robbers, 20
Gums, 56, 60. *See also* mummy, mummification, resin.

Hands, 58, 60
Hair, 58
Harp, 39, 66
Harvest, 18
Head, 62. *See also* skull.
Heart, 42, 43, *43*, 47, 53, 55, 56. *See also* "Weighing of the Heart."
Heavenly Fields, 35, 42, *42*
Hieratic, 47
Hieroglyphs, *iii*, 19, 30, 47, 55, 65, 73
Horus, 22, 24, 26, 59, 69
"House of Eternity," 1, 58. *See also* tomb.
"House of Purification," 49, 62. *See also* "Beautiful House."
Hunefer, *25*, *70*

Internal organs, 56, 67. *See also* viscera.

Intestines, 53, 55, 56
Inundation. *See* Nile, flooding of
Iouiya, *58*, *64*, *65*
Irrigation, 16, 17, 18
Ishtar, 23
Isis, 22, 23, 24, *25*, 66

Jewellers, 34. *See also* jewels.
Jewels, *53*, 66. *See also* collars, jewellers.
"Judgment of the Dead" ceremony, 42. *See also* ceremonies.

*Ka* (invisible twin), 26, 27, 30, 51
Karnak, Temple of Amun at, 8, 12, 13
Khnumbaf, 45–47
Kidneys, 53, 55

Lamb, 37. *See also* food.
Leeks, 37.
Lentils, 37.
Libations, 66. *See also* ceremonies.
Linen, 16, 24, 37, 56, 59, 60, 62, 68. *See also* agriculture, embalming, mummy.
Lips, 69. *See also* "Opening of the Mouth" ceremony.
Litter, 1, 2, 20, 37
Liver, 53, 56
Lower Egypt, 4, *5*
Lungs, 53, 55, 56

Lute, 39

Luxor, 71; temple at 10, *11. See also* Thebes.

Maat (goddess), 43

Mask, mummy, 62, *64*

Mason (of tomb), 49

Mastabas, 20

Mayet (sister-in-law of Ramose), 31, 32

Meat. *See* food.

Medicine, practice of, 47, 48

Medicines, 48

Mediterranean Sea, 16, 23

Memnon, Colossi of, *8–9, 9*

Memphis, 10

Men (sculptor), 28. *See also* sculptors.

Meritptah (wife of Ramose), 1, 22, 26, 27, 33, *33*, 34, 70

Merytamun, *53*

Mesopotamia, 71

Metalworkers, 34

Mitanni, 6

Mond, Sir Robert, 71

"Mortuary Liturgy" ceremony, 22. *See also* ceremonies.

Mortuary temple, 9

Mouth. *See* "Opening of the Mouth" ceremony.

Mummification, 49, 50, 51, *51*, 52, 56, 58, 62. *See also* mummy.

Mummy, 24, 34, 43, *53*, 56, *58*, 60, *61*, 62, *63*, 64, 65, 69, 71, 73

Musicians, *39*, 69. *See also* harp, lute.

Mutemwiya, Queen, 6

Myrrh, 59. *See also* spices.

Nails, 58

Nakht (tomb of), *19, 38, 39*

Narmer, Palette of, *5*

Natron, 55, 56, 58, 59

Neb-maet-ra Amenhotep. *See* Amenhotep III

Nebamun and Ipuki (tomb of), *frontispiece*, *50*

Neby (father of Ramose), 30, 31, *31*

Neck, 64

Nefertiti, Queen, 12, *14*, 29, *29*, 40

Nepthys (goddess), 24, 66

New Kingdom, 6

Nile, 1, *2–3*, 4, 9, 12, 16, 20, 23, 24, 36, 37, 40, 41, 49, 62, 65, 68, 71; flooding of, 16, 17, 19

Nostrils, 59

Nubia, 34

Nut (goddess), 56, 65

Oil, 59, 66, 69. *See also* gums, resin.

Ointments, 59. *See also* oil, resin.

Onions, 16, 59. *See also* agriculture, food.

"Opening of the Mouth" ceremony, 22, 26, 60, 69, *70. See also* ceremonies.

Osiris, 22, 23, 24, *25*, 42, 43, 44, 51, 59, 69; legend of, 22ff., 26

Painters, 28, 32, 49
Pairy (tomb of) *68*
Papyrus, 22, 45, 47
Peas, 37. *See also* food.
Perfume, 66
Per-Nefer. *See* "House of Purification."
Per-Nefer, Master of Works, 28
Pharaoh, 1, 4, 6, 12, 13, 15, 28, 34
Phoenicia, 23
Pomegranates, 38
Pork, 37. *See also* food.
Porphyry, 52
Ptah, 10
Pumpkins, 37. *See also* food.
Pyramids, 20

Radishes, 37. *See also* food.
Resin, 56, 59, 60. *See also* mummy, oils.
Robbers, 70

Salt, 37, 48, 55
Sandals, 60
Sarcophagus, 1, 21, 34, 70. *See also* coffin.
Scarab, 53, 55, 62

Scribe, 19, 26, 43, 45, 47, 52; scribe's palette and brushes, 66
Sculptors (also called "enliveners"), 28, 32, 49
Seasons (Germination, Inundation, Warm), 19
Sennodem (tomb of), *42*, *51*
Seth, 22, 24, 26
Seti I, *61*
Shawabtis, *35*, 35, 67
Silk, 37
Silver, 34, 65
Sinai, 34
Sirius (star), 19
Sitamun, Queen, 10
Skin, 58, 60
Skull, 52, 59. *See also* head.
Sledge, 65, 67, 68, *68*
Smenkhkare, 72
Sodium carbonate, sodium bicarbonate, 55
Sodium chloride, 55. *See also* salt
Sphinx, 9
Spices, 55, 56, 59. *See also* embalming.
Spinach, 37. *See also* food.
Stomach, 53, 56
Stuart, Villiers, 71
Sun, 55; disk, 13
Syria, 23

Tell El Amarna, 13–14, *14*, 72
Teye, Queen, 10, *11*, 73

Thebes, 1, 10, 12, 13, 15, 28, 37, 44, 50, 66
Thoth (god), 43
Thutmosis (infant), 10
Thutmosis I (Pharaoh), 20
Thutmosis IV (Pharaoh), 4, 6
Toes, 58, 60, 62
Tomb, 6, 9, 20, 21, *21*, 27, 28, 34, 59, 69, 70, 71. *See also* "House of Eternity."
Touiyou, *57*, *58*, *64*, *65*, 73
Tutankhamun, *27*, 40, *41*, *61*, 72
Tutankhaten, 40, 72. *See also* Tutankhamun.
Tuya. *See* Touiyou.

Underworld, 41
Upper Egypt, 4, *5*, 16

Valley of the Kings, 9, 20
Vegetables, 37, 66. *See also* food.
Viscera, 53, 55, 56, *57*

Vizier, 1, 4, 12, 15, 16, 28, 30, 32, 34, 45, 49

Walking stick, 66
Wall painting, *frontispiece*, *19*, *39*, *42*, *50*, *51*, *67*, *68*, 71
Wax, 59 *See also* gums, resin.
"Weighing of the Heart" ceremony, 42–43, *43*. *See also* ceremonies.
Wheat, 16. *See also* agriculture, food.
Wife of Ramose. *See* Meritptah.
Wine, 38, *38*, 39, 50, 55, 56, 66, 69
Woodworkers, 36
Wool, 37
Wrapping, 62. *See also* bandages.

Yalu, Fields of. *See* Heavenly Fields.
Yupuya (mother of Ramose), 31, *31*
Yuya. *See* Iouiya.

*Designed by Kohar Alexanian*
*Set in 12 pt. Avanta*
*Composed and bound by The Haddon Craftsmen, Inc.*
*Printed by The Murray Printing Company*
HARPER & ROW, PUBLISHERS, INCORPORATED